Home Fires:
20 poems 4 2012

Boni Sones OBE

New works for The Jubilee and London 2012 Olympics

GW00689996

Home Fires: 20 poems 4 2012

A sequel to *The Mermaid's Tale – A Portrait of Suffolk*
and *Two Mermaids Together* – published in October 2009.
And my three other companion works *All4Now*, *Food on the Table
All in One* and *Dear Alex All in One*, all published in January 2012.

ISBN   978-0-9565871-6-9

First published December 2012 by www.bonisonesproductions.com

Front cover photograph © Tanya Barnard
Back cover photograph © Tanya Barnard

Photographs on pages 2, 7,11 and 13 © Tanya Barnard
Photograph on page 4 © Caroline Adams
Photographs on pages 9, 15 and 18 © Boni Sones

Printed by Print-Out, Histon, Cambridge CB24 9JE

Contents

Introduction – New Beginnings and Acts of Reciprocity

Family life blossomed for many of us in 2012 with the coming out into our streets for the Jubilee celebrations and then the London 2012 Olympic Games. These "20 Stories From The Home Fires 4 2012" continue a theme of my writing for many years of the love of family, and friends, god-children and just "talking" and being together. What fun!

So often those little acts of togetherness go unrecorded in an age of the relentless reporting of global brutality yet I am sure that companionship, love, and those very small acts of reciprocity that pass between us all on a daily basis need to be "reported" too. From my own front-line, from my own desk and my own room with a view, looking out onto the garden and autumn trees leaves falling I bring you my more "mundane" news of my family and friends. When much isn't sustainable, reciprocity still is.

Hot foot from my Wednesday's reporting of women in politics from Central Lobby in Westminster I often reflect on how the sword fight and shouting at Prime Minister's Questions can seem out of touch with the more sensitive realities of our own lives.

I hope these 20 small poetic records of my year perhaps resonate more accurately the personal realities around the "Home Fires" of every-day life for most of us particularly as we experience deep grief for those we have lost – humans and animals, it seems! There is always a sting in a Suffolk Tale, so read on!!

Pauline at the Arts in April showers

We agreed to meet for the afternoon showing
A Moscow Bolshoi ballet
"The Bright Stream"
There was spring in Pauline's step
It was Spring
2012
And excitement in her voice
She was dazzled
Sparkled
In delight at the dancing
A programme to put imagination into the Spring air
Imagination "just think" or "you would have thought that?",
Nothing but pleasure and delight at what her eyes had seen and her eyes
had heard
And her mind now imagined
We both came out of the Arts in Cambridge dancing in our head
And then supper and the stories
"chit and chat, chit and chat, this and that, this and that, chit and chat".
I tried out a couple of stories on Pauline,

She listened, thought and replied "…but Boni perhaps that…?"
And I thought and listened too: "Perhaps she is right on this one…."
Perhaps is such a good word, time for reflection … "perhaps"!
Not really an opinion but a listening tone,
On our platter on the table the food was in the mind not on the plate
"Food in the mind, food in the mind…!"
The Lucian Freud exhibition gets Pauline's rave review
Not so David Hockney: "all those tall trees"
A Spring afternoon with Pauline at the Arts
A friend who "delights" in the Arts….

A poem by text
Your shoreline home

Can you hear the waves roar?
roll as they crash to shores edge
Can you feel the splash on your feet
Sands pebbled shoreline rolls in
Tides edge
calls to heavens ascent
washed ashore
Home on beachcombers back
roll in dreams roll onto shoreline
We build our dreams on your swishing and sloshing rolling back today.
xxx

To Hilary

...and their fingers met on the keys
Piano duo
Fingers skipping
A moments distance apart
Separating notes of music time
Dance fingers dance
Play the keys – stroke the melody
Fingers compatible by a moments time
His then Hers
Hers then His
Moments music on Her piano
In tune they play their Jubilee notes
A moments space divides their fingers
Note hopping Skipping in tune
A moments distance in love to play
Piano duo for four hands two players
One guest!!! Xxx

We made Pinot Fizz – Jubilee Day

..We made pinot grigio Fizz
Champagne flowed as our river view windows newly cleaned shone boats
1000 vessels came past our window view
Friends and family around us
Riverview apartment
Jubilee boats line past us
Canoes motorboats barges cruisers
Sail boat sail
Winds tide on rivers back
Grey blowy waters
Wet rowers
And high crowds gathering spirits
Queen and all
Board at our nearby Harbour
We drink and eat – wave those red white and blue flags
Hug and say hello
Hug and say farewell
Jubilee friends on tides back watching
1000 boats glide by
Two hours pass at our start line
And a voice tells us "they still haven't started yet'!
Two hours of watching 1000 boats glide by shouting waving on waves
back
Jubilee fun at Yours Today!!" xx

Lotty in her dress

Lotty has a Jubilee dress
Lotty is dressed in black and white
Her hair slide is red blue and white
A Jubilee Princess all turned out and turning heads today
The Jubilee of our eyes behold
She can process round the garden
Turn a somersault and cartwheel
Change attire and change back
Independent and carrying her outfits in her Lotty bag in the back of the
People Carrier
We the People, Lotty Amanda and I travelling to Suffolk
Jewel County of the Queen's Queen Dom
A Jewel in our Suffolk Crown today
Lotty on shores edge, running, jumping, leaping down steps at the Hall to
the seas edge
Amanda in pursuit in case she dives into the grey currents on our home
shoreline
Lotty the "catch" of our tides edge today,
Caught and brought back in a net to our People carrier round trip
200 miles the Jubilee Princess was transported
There and back
Beach outfit, and ducks on Aldeburgh's sailing lake
Lotty in beach shorts and T shirt and flip flops
Time to return
Home on the tide and slide in hair
Our Jubilee Princess is a jewel in our Crown today
On coastline, in car and on land, she's landed in our laps
Lucky travellers we three.

Jubilee Day Party 2012

The family sweep in
It's dropping in time for our Jubilee Party
Amhurst Home
4 all to drop in
Jubilee drop ins, Hilary, Amanda and Paul
Family too, Son and girlfriend in hand
They sweep in and we greet and hug
And then champagne in hand
Talking to Joan, the Committee of three who arranged the arrangements
Jubilee sips of champagne and sandwiches and the toast to Her Majesty
Fondness on the lawn at Amhurst grows
And we grow fond of it too
Three Hoorays for the Jubilee Queen and her Jubilee friends on the front
lawn today
Hooray!!

Paradise Javelin ride

...There were fireworks in the air,
Pop, bang!
A white fairy walking a tightrope suspended from a motorbike
Fireworks at the closing ceremony of London 2012 Paralympics
A Sunday evening mellow yellow fields passed by on the train there
The Stratford Stadium newly built
The cable car crossed the Thames and TJ snapped pixs in the setting sun
"Snap, snap" the pictures taken we then look at the glory she has captured
Glory in the camera lens at London 2012, Glory in the Opening Ceremony with family and friends
Glory "bang" the fireworks explode over our heads
As Coldplay sing to us of "Para, Paradise, Para, Paradise"
A Javelin train ride from Kings Cross to Stratford and home again from Stratford to Cambridge
Athletes parading with medals, songs sung, fireworks crackling
"BANG!" "CRACK"!
Off again they go
And the four seasons ceremony: cyclists alight with flames in the Olympic Stadium at Stratford,
Scarecrows burning and dark with menace, "Chitty bang, bang" cars and festival goers
And snowflakes, white and paper dropping on our heads and bodies as we stand "swaying" in another "wave" that flows around the Stadium to our bodies tunes
London 2012 and parading Paralympians in front of us
A pop concert and hope and love surround us
The volunteers still there to ask and direct us to and from and safely home again,
I text as I reach and sit on the Cambridge train at Kings Cross
"Javelin amasing, here in 25 minutes from Stratford! Not bad"
Looking at her photos now, of them, of us, of her, of me, and thinking of the fun we have had
I dance in my head, memories content for years to come,
She so thoughtful got the tickets on line to the closing, close, of the London 2012 Games,
What memories to speak of for generations to come, I lock them away, safely stored in my memory chest, are you sitting

comfortably....Now I will begin......

Down the family line the stories will travel......as superfast as the Javelin train.....we all arrived on time! With love......

And definitely this sea of stories has no ending...

Pauline in Sunlight September 2012

It was a sunlit day
On the Thames Estuary
Strolling
Pauline...yes Paulineee
Hunt
Of the Cambridge Evening News
And our news was being updated!
A post Olympics London 2012
Thames Estuary Open London
Stroll
Along
Water's Edge
Tides waves
Floods gates
With others
London Engineers explaining the philosophy of
The Flood gates
The Thames Estuary
And the Tides
She wore a bag
Her stroll was easy
Her talk engaging and intelligent
Thoughtful as ever
On the train Paulineeee produced
The Telegraph
A writer's tribute to her Mother and the grief of her loss
My loss too now
And Pauline brought it from her bag to help me engage with my
personal grief too
Ever Thoughtful, every reading, ever ready
Pauline.....eeee
A day's memory remembered willow trees, rivers edge,
Tales of the Estuary
Her easy stroll, her easy manner, so easy to get lost in conversation
with Pauline
Her listening skills, and family too, updates of friends,
A companion to all stories, our stories joined as one now in
conversation

Past, present and future
What weather! What luck! What views, and how very clever of Pauline
To "bag" us a ticket for the Open London stroll,
Never, no NEVER to be forgotten! Our Olympic journey, London
2012 now complete
Pauline!

The Engagement Party – October Nights

Dear Lynda
The fire was lit on the patio
"The boys"
Drink in one hand
Friends close by
Talk of times old and present
"The boys" friends together on the patio
Talk of school...college...jobs..and now "The Engagement"!
Ed and Kate
Together forever
Kate and Ed
Her friends and his
Families too ..Lynda Jim and Mum and Dad
Together families
Trusted friends memories of each to the other
Moira's love hearts stand tall as cakes on sticks
A food on the table
Fizz and jukebox celebrations
The home fires burning by white sofas and a chair that swivels round
Whizz Bang Fizz the fireworks rocket sky high
Amy and Stuart next
Two cakes side by side brother Ed and sister Amy
Launched! Rocket into stars now their love is in the sky..
Rocket High hearts on sticks launched together into the heavens
And grandparents too sit on our shoulders with them in this space
Families love
Whizz Bang stars in the sky
For Ed and Kate
Sharing their love today
Loves hearts on sticks
Lynda and Jim's place
Kate's family embracing us too
Fizz into Fizz into Fizz
Champagne Love hearts on sticks and fireworks!
Fizz love launched today round the fire embers on the patio in the garden!
Starry nights of sun climates capture our imaginations
As Kate and Ed and Amy and Stuart cut their Engagement cakes

Diamond rings sparkle on wedding fingers
"Ahhh those summer nights....s"!
Greece Lightening loves
To Ed and Kate "those summer nights...s"!
XX lovers two!!

Diamond fingers – the Engagement sequel

XX We saw in your diamond fingers rainbows dancing to stars light
Rainbows of jukebox music
"The boys" round fires light
and music tunes sending rhythms dreams star high
Music in nights air
creating rainbow family rooms
Aunts Uncles cousins
New ones too
In fireworks bang
Love explodes by fires light
in nights glow
And loves rainbows appear
generations shadows dance with us in moons glow
Relatives returned now gone
Come to our sides today
We feel their charm and hands to hold by ours...they join us too..
rainbows pastel shades blue yellow green violet
tell of loves pledge
Amy Stuart
Kate and Ed
Diamond rings
sparkle
Bang Fizzz
Moonstruck by firelight
And families loves renewed in their hands
Fizz Bang....warm patio nights
Look to the stars
Rainbow love in fireworks trail
The Red Arrows fly by
tail flight "Kate and Ed" we read in the lights dancing in the sky
The Engagement Party at the parents pad tonight!
"Those Summer Nights....s"! X

Ali rings the bells!

She stands at the top of the Tower
Ringing advice into our ears
Ali
Ali Rings
Ringing the ringer's tunes
ensuring no snags or snarls,
the ropes
dangling
tied
"Hands on the Sally
Look to the Treble
She's gone!"
We ring
Ali watches...
then dashes to my side
Safe
In Ali's hands...
There is no need to abandon the Bells
Ali's at our side
A friend in ringing
bringing to us
what she learnt in her youth
London 2012 Bell ringing tower tours
Histon, Cottenham, Willingham, Longstanton,
Ali's Canterbury friends cycle with us
Towers ringing out
Ropes
And Ringers
Paul, Penny, Liam, Marie, Peter, Lea, Tim.....and more
Ali's done this for us
And now I compose her birthday poem
Ring words Ring
Ring those words from tower to tower
Ring thanks to Ali
Ali Ring
On her Birthday
Please Ali Please
Can we ring a round for you?
Ding Bong Ding Bong Ding Bong

We've celebrated hands on our Sally's
"Looking to the Treble
And now she's gone!"
Happy Birthday Ali
And now a rich dark chocolate Brownie
is being baked for you
Come round soon
Ding Bong Ding Bong Ding Bong
Happy Birthday to You
Ali
Ali Ring!

Somersaults

....now grown
I turn Somersaults when I think of you
standing on my head now
I can see you from the ground up
Now grown
I flip my legs over my head
And Somersault
At the thought of you
A hand-stand
Birds eye view from the ground
of how tall you are now
hand in hand you travel
By your side a love of your life
And upside down I view those travels
A Somersault when I think of you
And your old cast-off jumper
Holes in sleeves
Keeps you close by nights fall
Close and standing upside down I have now
A birds-eye view of you
So tall
So Grown
So Fabulous as I flip
Flip, jump, flip
Head on the floor
Legs in the air
Your jumper now with holes
Brings you closer to me! X

She thinks she's a dog

Bark
A dog
Wolf Wolf
She thinks she's a dog
And we all bark too..
In the cage of the floor
She growls and crawls
Around in her cage
Refusing to come out
So we put the plate on the floor and watch for her to put her paw out
Wolf
She's a dog a dog and we call to her "Lotty dog, Lotty dog" come out
Growl, sniff, growl, crawl, bark, walk,
Lotty IS a dog, for sure, for sure, Lotty IS a dog,
Growl bark on the floor in her cage…stroke her now, keep her warm,
and bring nice chocolates to her feet
Lotty Dog at home today!

The Bubble Girl

Lotty in bubbles
She was a girl in a bath tub
A bath tub of bubbles
Surrounded by a sea of sparkling water
Rising and falling the bubbles washed over
A tiny six year old
In her bathtub of bubbles
How she chatted and made fun
Told all how often she blew bubbles
How to blow bubbles
And what fun it was to blow bubbles from your mouth
Lips pursed
Bubbles and Lotty
Bathtub of joy
The fun of being six in a Tub of her own
She sat the Queen of bubbles in her bathtub today
Blowing bubbles as she sat in bubbles
Bubbles of fun told stories to those around her
Bubble Lotty aged six!

Edgy now

Edgy now
He drives a fast car
And lives by the side of a Common
In a large apartment
Edgy now
He has a partner
They cook for us
Family four
Stew with dumplings
Edgy now
A slide show of Africa and tigers and growls
And camp fires and drinks
A girlfriend on his arm
Edgy now
His phone calls come quick and crackly and he talks soooo fast
Edgy now
He listens a touch more than he used to
Edgy now
A son
Thirty something
At home on sofa new with his girlfriend
Edgy now
Fast then slow then fast then slow
A home of his very own
Edgy son and stew and dumplings
Hooray for his new Friend!

Four poems written at a November Concert

You could feel the notes
Flowing mid air
Reaching a crescendo
The Concert ended
Movement's time spent playing
Together
An Orchestra playing
Beethoven
Inspiration flowing
Four poems from fingers spring....

Advising

I probably advised you to leave
When you wanted no needed to stay
I probably gave the wrong advice
At the wrong time
Said the wrong words
To loves withering vine
I must have said and done the wrong thing
And then you left
Recovery
Rebirth
Forgive my feeble attempts to move you on
New home
Plans
I know I said the wrong thing
But you did leave!

Central Lobby

We stand in Central Lobby
Talking
My microphone recording
Your answers
We stand asking and answering
Questions
Of importance
We stand talking
On Wednesday in Central Lobby

Elderflower Fizz

It sparkled
Elderflower Fizz went pop
When the party should have ended
It began again
Nights fall brought new guests
reborn by Peta's Elderflower Champagne
After dessert it was served
We drank it in our now empty champagne glasses
At desserts served end
The Food on my Birthday Table served
Chocolate dark and light Profiteroles
But then what surprise we began all over again
Turkey venison and beef
Cheeses too
But chocolate profits
Eaten
Out then came the sugar filled elderflower champagne
And fond friends became even louder this time their party chatter all over
again
Peta laughed when I asked what made the elderflower so sparkly
Why had they queued in my kitchen for more?
"Loads of sugar and just one part elderflower"
Came the reply
Champagne elderflower ending to party talk this July 6 Birthday
Peta' s Suffolk feast. Yum. X

Dispatched

Dispatched
Elsie came home in procession
Dispatched
An old friend and pal
who walked side by side
Dispatched
heaven bound
passing peacefully
By best friend's side
Her dog
Dispatched
A hole dug by home
Elsie rests with them
Dispatched
At home
At rest
peaceful friends passing
still side by side Elsie
A dog who knew when her owner was coming home!

The gaps in our memories time cast for Miriam

She left us

Time travels by her side today
Her spaces now inhabited by memories
Thoughts travel each day to her side
The spaces between memories
Leave gaps

A huge void mountains high and sea wide
And tides roar and splash on stormy shores
When the full moon shines I think of her romance
Her dancing feet, her need of love
And mischief
The spaces she leaves stab heart bound piercing flesh and denting bones
Rearranging bodies interior
She's left

Gone
Spirit high
And the leaving creates storms, floods, famine, earthquakes and fire
A wound bleeding today
Patching up patching up...
Her leaving tears flesh
And memories dance now to her tunes to her feet to her "Food on the
Table"
Love never meets burns fires to quell
Her dancing feet, her mischief, her fondness and her soft skin
Old now she still clings to our flesh to our soul
To our memories time warn now
Piercing our flesh and giving us life, renewed, again
"Food on our Table" once more.....storms, storms, storms, shores waves,
seas edge,
Fish and lobster, fish and lobster hands on the table,
Miriam's hands sing to us a beach and ocean on our plates,
Knives and forks at the ready
"Food on the Table", blow wind blow, blow Miriam back to our shores
today
Rush her to us on your wave's back, bring her riding high on your tide
To us

Gone, piercing white shafts of shrapnel fired from the cannons on our
beaches
All memories, times lapses, come crashing in and out of our memories
now
In and out
Times worn tides and sands beaches, lobsters, shrimps and fishes
Miriam's hands and "Food on the Table" a slow year, of fond memories,
of farewells not said
She's gone

Tears on oceans back and tides winds shed
She's gone

Time casts her nets on waves back, fish her back, fish her back, fish her
back to us,
But on that grey cast sea we can see her now in gorse, yellow blossom,
On Tides shore and beach's sandy back,
She's gone
Home now
We are you see, still "Miri's girls"!

Epilogue

One last inside back-page story taken from my previous work *The Mermaid's Tale:* "My Dad and the Love of the Piggy Back". I seem to listen to him more now that he has gone and her too – the child still whining for just one my goodnight story from Bert and another roast parsnip from Miriam!

My dad and the love of the piggy back:

"In our small house the story was always preceeded by the piggyback. Climbing the fourteen stairs to the first-floor bedroom, in darkness, was the scariest part of the day. "Piggyback me", we whined after taking out the ribbons from his hair. We regularly stood behind him, as he sat in the chair reading his paper, combing his hair, creating hairstyles until he retorted that he was sure to go bald, if we spent another night playing hairdresser with him. He did develop a round bald patch in the middle of his head, and sought guidance from the Readers Digest on how to remedy this daughter induced baldness. The Readers Digest was always proclaiming a "New Miracle Cure for Baldness". He cut them out and kept them. The hairdressing ritual always then led to the piggyback up the stairs. "Pick me up, let me climb on now", we pleaded as he stooped down to transport us one at a time up the winding dark stairs. Paraffin lamps lit the kitchen, but you climbed the stairs in darkness until you reached your bedroom, where more lamps lit the room. The piggybacking was always the most delicious ritual of the day. Daily it was performed and daily we never stopped clambering for more. "Me first, me first", we pleaded and whined, and once at the top of the stairs, he tucked us into bed and began reading the story. Warm and cosseted we knew we were safe. ..."